How to Fight (and Win) Anything!

By Rebecca Robinson

Minute Help Press
www.minutehelpguides.com

© 2011

Table of Contents

Auctions

Auctions have always been exciting and promising places to make purchases, and they have never been more relevant to the public than in the present day. With the surge of auction sites across the Internet, there are more possibilities to buy items online than ever before.

Websites like eBay.com have become among the leading marketplaces on the Web, and are hugely popular places to buy and sell goods. They have also, however, prompted a number of issues that most people new to auctions might run into – and chief among these has been the propensity for beginners to want to back out of an auction.

If you are trying to get out of an auction that you bid for an eBay, this can possibly be a tricky process. Backing out of an auction that you have won will create a tense situation between you and the seller, and it should be handled with care. If you were irresponsible with your eBay bid, and have no genuine reason for backing out of the bid, you may have to be a bit dishonest or deceptive to get out of the bid. If this is your case, you may follow three methods that will likely get you out of paying for a won item on any of the major bid websites.

You may do this if you bid on an item one day, and then see it advertised elsewhere on an auction site – or in the Sunday papers – for a much lower price. You might just want to back out, especially if you have already spent the money on the other item.

When this happens, just as with a live auction, there is no real way to "back out" without cause. The auctions are legal and binding, and you will have to find the rare exceptions to the rule. One such exception can be found in a winning bid that you accidentally placed.

If you priced your bid wrong on accident, you can usually get out of the bid rather easily. This may be your case, and if it is, you may have no problem. If you are only saying that your bid was placed incorrectly, it may be more difficult to prove. If you bid $100.00 for an item that is clearly not worth that much – and your intended bid was $10 – you will not find much trouble in admitting that you listed your bid incorrectly. If, however, you have to lie and say you bid too high on an item that is worth close to your bid, you may have to present that you didn't know the true worth of the item, or that you thought to the item to be worth what you "meant" to bid.

You can also try to claim that the item that you won is significantly different or altered from the item that was received, or that you were led to believe it would be different. Again, this may take some selling of your points, especially if you are being dishonest.

Your third option is to hope that the seller can no longer be contacted, or somehow make it so that you cannot contact the seller – and that you can prove it. If this is your case – or any of the previous two scenarios – you should be able to fight your way out of paying for the item.

Jury Duty

Jury duty is one of those annoying processes that nearly every American will have to go through – or get called for – some time in their life. Many creative people wishing not to serve during a trial, however, have found ways to get out of jury duty. They have used these ways to stay out of the courtroom, and rid their lives of the annoyance of taking off of work, getting the measly jury pay and wasting boring hours in trial proceedings.

While not showing up for jury duty could land you in jail, there are ways to either stop yourself from getting selected, or to limit your actual duty to one short day. The following are realistic and more fun ways of getting out of jury duty, and most are rather fool proof in allowing you to avoid the undesired task.

You could begin by demonstrating to the court that you are financially unable to serve on the jury. If you cannot afford to get the days off of work, to get babysitters for your children, to take extra days off and to leave your projects unattended for an extended period – you may be granted leave from duty by a judge. You should bring supporting documents such as pay stubs, tax forms and bank account information.

Indicate a requested change of date on the computerized jury duty form. You can indicate that you are ill, or planning a vacation out of the country, studying for your law exams or joining the military. Any well thought up and reasonable excuse can allow you to push your duty back as far as a year.

Your next tactic for avoiding jury duty can be found in the practice of simply playing smart or playing dumb in court. As the trial begins, you can act like you already know everything there is to know about the case and the issues at hand. Coming in equipped with knowledge of the case will disqualify you for a spot on the jury. Likewise, if you simply know quite a bit about education, law, reasoning and other subjects involved in the case, you may be barred from duty because of your prerequisites.

While you are asked to submit your verdict based on the law at hand, and not your feelings, you should question whether a judge would have upheld or ruled against famous Americans like Harriet Tubman or Rosa Parks, who were found in violation of American laws at the time. You can also play stupid, and pretend that you are either racist, prejudiced, a know-it-all or seemingly above the laws of the court. You can tell the judge that you could spot a guilty person by following your gut, and you will have a good chance of being let off of the jury due to your inability to rule properly.

Lease

Leases are a big part of life for people all around the world, and they can play a large part in affecting your day-to-day financial situations. The most common type of lease – besides for your vehicle – is an apartment lease, and these will determine where you live and how long you live there.

If you are stuck in a lease that you signed for too long of a time period, you may find yourself getting restless and frustrated at your current living situation. You may have found a cheaper place, a better location or you may simply want to get out of your agreement. If this is the case, and your lease is not yet up, there are a number of things that you can do to get out of your apartment lease.

The first step, and perhaps the most amicable, is to negotiate a lease-break agreement. This type of agreement gives you the chance to agree with the superintendent or landlord to get out of the lease early, and will specify what you have to do to break that contract. You could offer to return some of the deposit, to pay for a few months after you vacate or to find a new tenant to fill the room that you are leaving.

Next, and this may be a deceptive way of getting out of your lease, you can find something in your apartment that is dangerous or defective. If there is a true safety concern in your apartment, and if it is something that the landlord may not be able to do anything about, you will be able to get out of the lease without a new agreement. These conditions can include mold, broken detectors and loose railings.

Your next option is to determine that your apartment does not look like the model that you were showed when you signed your lease agreement. If this is the case, you can declare Deceptive Trade Practices and you might be able to get out of your lease this way. If you were made to sign a lease for a room that you were not expecting, you might not be obligated to uphold your end of the lease.

Alternately, you can decide that your complex is unsafe or not secure. Just as with something broken in your apartment, if the gates outside of the complex are broken, or if the parking lot for the apartments is unsafe, you may be able to declare that you fear for your safety. This can give you a prime chance to get out of your lease, especially if the landlord is liable and if no action is taken immediately.

Make sure you know who your landlord is when you are renting an apartment as well. Or, in this case, you can do your best to avoid learning the identity of the management company or owner of the complex. Because this information must be disclosed to you, failure to do so can give you an out on your apartment lease.

Air Fare

Flying has become one of the top methods of transportation around the world, but for many it is also one of the most expensive. One way of getting around the price of expensive tickets is by purchasing discounted tickets when they are on sale. Because of the nature of these tickets, they are often listed as non-refundable.

In most cases, airlines will stick to this policy, and it can be nearly impossible to get a refund on your non-refundable ticket. When this happens, you may be stuck paying the price of your plane ticket, even though you are not flying, and this can be a large financial drain.

There are, however, things that you can try, and there is a chance that these may work to get you out of paying for your non-refundable tickets. If you do not get the full price of the ticket refunded, you will likely at least get around paying the full price of the ticket for the flight.

You can first attempt to contact the customer service department of the airline that you plan on flying with. Once in contact with customer service, you can get in touch with a representative to explain why you are unable to use the tickets. Emergencies will work in many cases, such as unexpected illnesses and deaths, but these are not the conditions under which you will be likely to have trouble fighting your non-refundable airfare.

You could also ask to speak to a supervisor of the customer service department, and depending on the representative and the branch, you may be able to talk them into issuing you a refund for your ticket for a minor reason. You could also try to negotiate them into transferring your ticket to a future flight, giving you credit with the airline, or reducing the price of your non-refundable ticket. You may be able to talk them down to as low as $50 or $75 for your ticket.

You can also get out of your ticket if you have jury duty, if you have been served with a subpoena or if you are attending jury duty. You will need to provide documentation for these, but they will work to allow you to leave your ticket unused and not have to pay for it.

One more method of getting a refund for a non-refundable ticket can be more difficult, but can be used in two separate situations. If you are being denied access to the plane for security reasons, make sure that you get an official statement of your reason. If the reason was unjust, you can submit this reason to the airline and get a legal refund for your non-refundable ticket.

If you have not been removed from the flight, you can hope to get searched by security – or so something inconspicuous that might pique the interest of security. You can then deny to be searched, and you will be led out of the airport. If it was not found that there was a reason for denying you flight or requesting a search, you will be able to get your refund for your ticket price.

Hotels

Hotels are stayed in throughout the world by billions of people every year. If you are traveling, and you are not staying with friends or family, there is a good chance that you will be staying at a hotel.

Many hotels, like airlines and other resources, offer discounted and cheaper rates that can be purchased in advance. These rates are, however, often tagged with the term "Non-refundable," and they require a degree of commitment to your vacation or to your plans.

If you have had to cancel a trip or a night's stay at the last minute, it can be quite difficult for you to cancel your non-refundable hotel room. If this is the case, there are a number of things that you can try. These methods, however, will not be exactly fail-proof.

You can change your reservations practice first. Instead of booking non-refundable rooms, you can book a refundable room that can be cancelled. Then, a few days before your reservation, you can attempt to book the non-refundable rate and cancel the normal rate.

If it is already too late for you to use this method, you can call the hotel chain and talk to a customer service representative. While natural disasters, illness or injury, emergencies and excrescent circumstances will most likely allow for a refund, many other situations will not. You could take your chance and ask, and depending on the representative or the hotel, you may be granted your request for a lesser reason.

You can also attempt to make it to your hotel, and hope that the room is different than the one that you requested, or that something essential is missing. If this is the case, you will be able to get out of your reservation and get your refund because of their deceptive practices.

You can also get out of the refund if things in your room are unsafe, or if there is something wrong with the hotel – such as faulty safety or security practices. If any of these are the case, you may easily be able to cancel your reservation and get your money back.

You can also try to call your credit car company, tell them that the credit card was stolen, and have the card canceled. You will be unable to use your card and the company will have to send you a new one, but the hotel will likely by unable to charge your card with the price of the hotel.

Grades

Everyone is affected by the grades they get in school – whether it is during college or high school. These grades will determine the college that you get into, and the jobs that you will be getting once you leave college.

Your grades are a reflection of your preparation and your ability to do work and learn things, and they are the final word on your competency.

If you are achieving low marks in your classes, you might find that your grades are doing less than meeting your standards. If this is the case, you will either have to start working harder, or will have to petition your teachers or professors for the grade that you feel you deserved. You can do this in a number of ways, whether you deserve the better grade or not.

You can start by asking your professor for a grade review. If you think one is warranted, you can ask the professor to go over all of your points for the semester and determine why it is that you got your mark. You can make sure that all of the marks were fair and that the professor explains why they were given.

Your next step can be to make an appointment with your professor to determine how you got your grade, and what you can do to improve the grade, or to get better grades on your next assignment. You can ask the professor if there is a chance for extra credit, and you can also ask him how you can improve your performance for following assignments. You can explain that you did not understand the previous assignments, and ask if your grades can be changed retroactively once you prove that you understand and can complete the following assignments.

The next step you can take will be to appeal your grade with a higher level. You can go to the department head to see what can be done about your grade, or you can go to a dean, professor or director to see what actual grade you deserve.

Ask your professor if you can redo some of your past assignments, and ask them if your new grade or a percentage of your new grade can be applied to the old one. You can tell them that you misread the instructions, that you had personal issues that were distracting you from doing your best or you can try to defend your answers as actually being correct.

Suspensions

A suspension can be a nuisance for anyone in a high school or grade school, and this can ruin your semester or marking period. If you are suspended from school, you will likely miss at least one day, and this may affect your grade or your reputation with other teachers.

When you are suspended, it is used as a disciplinary measure due to something wrong that you did. Many who are suspended are absolutely averse to serving their suspensions, and there are a number of things that you can do to attempt to get out of your suspension. If you are trying to fight the suspension, here are some simple things that you can do to try to get out of it.

You should start by recognizing and recording all of the officially stated reasons for your suspension. If you can refute these reasons, and give adequate reasons why they are not true, you will be able to avoid your suspension.

You should prepare your suggestions for why the reasons listed are not true, and you should ask for a meeting with the person who administered the suspension. You must then try to convince the teacher, principle or administrator that the reasons that you were suspended for were not true.

You will have to appeal on the grounds that the decision that was made to suspend you was erroneous, and that the suspension was unjust in the first place. You should write down as much information about the circumstance as possible, and you should get as much information from other people as you can.

Find out how many other people the administrator or teacher has spoken with, and go out of your way to investigate the incident as closely as possible. You should understand exactly what the suspending party thinks happened, and then identify how what actually happened is different from what they think. Once you have done this, you should then state what you think an appropriate punishment would be, or declare why your punishment does not fit your actions.

You could also try to appeal using a written letter, and you could use your letter to explain why the school was overly harsh with the punishment, or how they did not treat similar situations with the same punishment. You could explain how the policy has not always been followed, or you can even detail how you or your child was not given due process. You can discount eyewitnesses or others involved in the incident, and can explain what should be done instead.

Workplace

The workplace is an interesting enigma in everyday life. If is one place that most people dislike as much as any, but it is the place where we spend roughly one-third of our lives. It is our workplaces that provide us with our livelihoods, and you use it to make money, to retire early, and to live the way you want to.

There are things at the workplace that people enjoy – such as fun projects, co-workers and interaction – but there are other things that seem like more of a hassle than they are worth. In your workplace, there are a number of things that may frustrate you, and these things are issues that you may have to fight over for a variety of reasons. If you are trying to get out of being punished or reprimanded, trying to argue for a higher salary or trying to fight to get time off, there are ways to do this that will allow you the best results possible.

To get time off from your job, you can point out a number of reasons or excuses for your boss or for your hiring department. You can provide some religious or family reason, you can argue that your performance will improve with some extra time off; you can point out your ability to complete all of your work faster if you can have some time off. There are a number of arguments you can make for receiving some extra time off.

If you are reprimanded by your boss or by a superior, you should respond calmly and give both yourself and your boss time to cool down from the situation. You can approach your boss by scheduling an appointment or meeting with him or her, and you can discuss the circumstances behind your reprimand. You should give your side of the story, and remain accountable for any mistakes that you have made. You should also not minimize the errors that you have made, but you should simply discuss them. You should realize why you were punished, and explain to your boss why the things that you did were not done the wrong way, or why they were justified. You can provide past example of similar acts, or you can argue why the punishment does not fit the crime.

You can offer other suggestions or solutions for your boss, and you should do all that you can to come up with a fairer punishment for your violation, instead of the current reprimand. You should understand fully the repercussions of what you did, and you should analyze entirely the listed reasons for your punishment.

Arguing or fighting for salaries is also a common practice at workplaces around the world, and if you are trying to get an increase in the money that you are making, there is a number of ways to go about this. This is as delicate a process as any in your career, and it can go a long way in determining the progress of your career, as well as how you are living at home. To fight for a higher salary, you can attempt to use a number of the following methods.

There are a number of things that you can do before you consider asking for a pay raise, and all of these things can better position you to be accepted for it. You can begin to work more overtime for your company, you can offer to be on-call for a few hours before and after every shift during the week, and you can offer to put in weekends or nights if required. You can also ask for special assignments, and make sure that your performance is up to the highest quality that it can be on the job.

Your first step in fighting for a higher salary can be doing your research. Your should make sure that you are familiar with what other people in your situation are making, and you should be sure to compare yourself to other positions, other locations and other companies. Be able to demonstrate how people in similar situations are making more, and do all that you can to show how you are doing more in your job than they are.

You can search the Bureau of Labor Statistics to make sure that you are making money commensurate to your experience and your education, and you should know what demand your skills are in. You should also make sure that you are setting up a face-to-face with your boss. You should prepare what you are going to say to your boss, and know how much you deserve to get increased.

You should always ask for more than you would like to get, so that there is room to negotiate down from there, and you could also consider alternatives to the money raise. You should ask for extra benefits, extra paid time off, extra vacations or extra overtime hours.

You are best off not blackmailing or threatening your boss, and you should dress neatly, act professionally and do your best to show your worth to your company. A truly worthwhile employee will be hard to find for many employers, and if you are good at what you do, you should know that the company will want to hang onto you.

You should apply for some other jobs and try to line up some interest with some other potential employers. You can try to find a higher job or one in a different location, and you should work to get an offer or some interest from these employers at a higher rate. If you have an offer for more money, or even some interest for more money, your boss will know that you are worth more, and you will have a better chance of getting more money in the form of a pay raise.

Parking Violations

Parking violations can be a headache for anyone. You can get a ticket or a violation for parking on the wrong street, in the wrong area or at the wrong time. If you are getting tickets for where and when you are parking, chances are you will have to pay a fine simply for leaving your car somewhere.

This can be a nuisance, especially if you parked your car for an emergency, just for a quick stop or because there were no other stops. If you are someone who gets a number of parking tickets, you probably work in a busy downtown area, and are likely parking in certain violation areas quite frequently.

While parking violations are much less serious than other tickets you might get, they can still set you back in the terms of payments, and you might find yourself paying over and over again if you are unsure why you are getting the tickets, or are unwilling to go out of your way to find a new place to park.

There are a variety of things that you can do to get out of these violations, but they may take some research, some work or some ingenuity. The first thing that you can do is analyze and review your ticket carefully. By doing this, you will know exactly why you were ticketed, where and when you were ticketed, and you will be able to determine if there are any factual errors or omissions on the ticket. If there are any mistakes on the ticket, you will likely be able to get out of the violation rather easily.

When you are in court attempting to fight your ticket, you should make sure that you are entirely honest with the judge. You should not attempt to lie or to cover anything up, and you should remember that judges will often recognize when you are lying.

You should also do your best not to attack the credibility of the officer that issued your ticket. In a fight with the cops they will win out almost every time, especially in the eye of the judge. You should provide evidence to support your claim that there was a mistake on the ticket, or that you were indeed not in violation of the infraction that you were charged with. If you can do either of these, it will likely be considerably easier to get the ticket dismissed.

The first thing you should look for is a mistake of fact. If you were ticketed for an incorrect time or incorrect location, and you can prove these things, the ticket will likely be thrown out and the case dropped. Likewise, if you can prove that the law enforcement officer does not have enough evidence against you, you will be able to get out of paying for the traffic infraction.

Another thing that can be done, which will often work with moving violations as well, is to contest the ticket at a time when the police officer who issued the ticket is likely to be engaged in something else. You should do what you can to discover the schedule of the police officer, and attempt to get a court date for a time when the police officer is on a shift in a different location. You should know why the cop will be most busy, and put yourself in a situation to where he or she will not show up in court. If the officer does not show up in court, the ticket will be thrown out and you will not be charged with the violation.

Conversely, you can attempt to get out of the ticket by simply showing that you are contrite or sorry for the circumstances of the violation. An attitude of contrition during your hearing with the judge and the law enforcement officer will give you an opportunity of the ticket having thrown out as well. If you are fully representing that you are aware of your mistake, and are sorry for it, you can also try to prove that there is no reason why the infraction should happen again. You should prove that you learned from your mistake, and you should know that doing all of these things will make the judge more inclined to be lenient with you. If the judge knows that you are going to try your best to do better in the future, they will be more likely to forgive or excuse this one violation.

In addition to finding mistakes on the ticket, you can also attempt to provide defending evidence against the circumstances of the ticket. You should look for unclear wording on the ticket, or you can find reasons why you may not have known that you could not park in a certain area. If the paint is too faded, if the wording on a sign is unclear and you thought you might be able to park there, a photograph might work to convince the judge that the violation was not deserved.

You can also attempt to bypass a ticket in a number of deceptive ways, and this may give you the opportunity to avoid getting the ticket in the first place. You can leave a hand-written note on your dashboard stating an emergency that required you to park there, or stating that the meter was not working. You can also leave your car in the spot with your emergency blinkers on and your hood popped. This will classify your vehicle as abandoned, and a busy officer may be less inclined to investigate or leave you a ticket in the situation.

You can also attempt to park on private property instead. You will not be able to be ticketed on this property, though if the police are called by the owner of the property there is a chance that you can get towed or that you will receive a citation.

How to Avoid and Beat Speeding Tickets

The red and blue lights are enough to make your hands shake. They'll make the sweat drip from your palms and your temples, and they'll get your blood pressure high. As soon as you hear the sirens, and see the car behind you, you feel like covering your head in your hands.

Even the brightest day on the sunniest street can be ruined by a simple traffic stop – and one that was avoidable to begin with. If you find yourself getting pulled over for speeding, your driving record, wallet and even habits behind the wheel can take a huge hit.

If you find yourself getting pulled over for speeding more than your family and more than your friends, you might not be taking advantage of certain things you can do to keep the red and blues away, and keep your breezing down the highways worry free.

Speeding tickets

A speeding ticket is not only an annoyance and a nuisance; it can also really devastate your home life, work life and social life in certain circumstances. Tickets, even for minor traffic violations of merely 5 miles per hour over the limit, can be as high as $75 to $100. These are compounded greatly, and even doubled and tripled, in the case of tickets given for going 10 miles per hour over the limit, or the dreaded reckless driving ticket, which is close to 15 miles per hour over the limit in most places.

If you are getting tickets often, you know the toll it can take on you financially. You can, however, avoid this toll, and eradicate the worry for your life. This will give you the freedom to drive how you like, give you the extra pocket cash to spend how you like, and keep you from feeling like pulling your hair out.

The toll of the tickets

Getting speeding tickets will not only cost you the price of the infraction, but will also cost you when you come to getting your car insurance. Just a few minor violations can boost your automotive insurance to as much as double what it used to be. Two five-over tickets can have you paying as much as $250 a month, depending on your car, and this is much more than the $100 than many people around the United States are paying.

In addition to higher auto insurance payouts, you may not be able to find the comprehensive coverage you like for your nice car, or will not be covered fully if you live in a dangerous area, or one with extended winters with excessive snow.

Your license can also take a hit, as each ticket can add one of two points to your driving record. With as little as six or eight points on your record, you can have your license suspended or revoked – and when this happens, you'll find yourself begging for rides, taking public transportation and doing anything you can to get out from under the embarrassment of not having a car. You might even relish the opportunity to be behind your own wheel, and even have the chance to risk seeing the red and blue lights behind you.

What to do during your traffic stop

There are a number of important things that you not only could do, but should do during your traffic stops. These things not only will put you in the best position to fight your ticket in court, they will also to help you beat the odds of not receiving the ticket on site in the first place.

When you are stopped by a police officer, certain protocols should be followed to ensure your safety, as well as the safety of the office and of other drivers on the road.

In addition to these safety protocols, there are a number of things you can do that will help you to achieve all or any of the following:

-avoid citations
-leave with a warning
-put the officer at ease
-prepare yourself for your defense in court

How to avoid citations

To avoid getting ticketed or cited after being pulled over is the tricky part. While you may think it is too late at this point, there are a number of things that you can still do to get yourself out of an annoying ticket or an expensive citation.

Perhaps the most important thing you can do is be polite, be courteous and answer questions when asked. But equally important is not being nervous or confused, knowing how to acquit yourself and making sure that you do not incriminate yourself or admit guilt.

You should never indicate what you may have been doing, and should never suggest with any answers that you may have been speeding.

Officers will often ask an open-ended question such as "Do you know why I stopped you?"

This question should never be answered with a statement that indicates that you were indeed speeding. Your answer should tell the officer that you do not know why you were pulled over; you can then go on to ask him why exactly he stopped you.

Next, you should be able to answer simple, non-incriminating questions with simple answers and without hesitations. These can include questions such as "Do you still live at this address?"

If an officer asks you if you know how fast you were going, or if you know what speed you were moving, this can be a tricky situation. You should know what kind of answers to give to portray that you did nothing wrong, and do not deserve a citation.

Tell the officer the following: "I was going at a safe and reasonable speed for the situation and the conditions in which I was driving."

Question the evidence or procedure

This may not make the officer happy, but if you are certainly getting a ticket it will not hurt to try to question the evidence or procedure used by the officer. This may take a level of memorization or knowledge, but there are some shady practices used by officers around the country that can make your citation null and avoid.

You can start by questioning the evidence. This can serve you one way by allowing yourself to be best equipped in court if you still get the ticket, but you can also bypass the ticket entirely if an officer agrees that he may be put in a precarious situation by giving you a ticket.

You can ask the officer how he determined your speed, and you can then ask questions like:

"When was your speedometer last calibrated? May I see proof of calibration?"
"May I see your tuning fork and calibration record?"
"When was the traffic and engineering survey last conducted? Was it within seven years? What speed did that survey yield for this stretch of the road and condition"?
"I can assume this is a speed trap, then?"

All of these questions may sound legal, and you may find an officer who does not have all the answers, or is made certain by these questions. If this is the case, they may let you go to spare themselves the hassle of having to address these questions on site or in court.

You can also indirectly try to question an officer if he is reaching a quota or if that position is established as a speed trap. If the officer acknowledges either fact, the ticket can be voided. Both quotas and speed traps are illegal, and these can trick the officer into letting you go.

You should ask the officer if they were allowed to give warnings, or were just here to write tickets. You can do a number of these things to try to make the officer less inclined to deal with a situation that may take longer than they had bargained for.

Fighting your traffic ticket

There are perhaps more ways to fight your ticket than any other step in the process, and this can be the most effective means of lowering your penalties, saving money, reducing insurance costs and saving the points that might be added onto your license.

You can fight tickets in a variety of ways, but you need to first have a general understanding of why this works, and the laws that will allow you to beat a ticket a majority of the time.

Just because you received a ticket doesn't necessarily mean that you deserved it, and there are a variety of tickets that are simply dismissed because officers are unable or are unwilling to show up in court for a simple traffic violation.

There are five main ways to fight tickets, and they are all viable options for most people who receive citations:

1. Challenge the officer's conclusion

This can be done for a variety of reasons or in a variety of ways, and is available as an option in many states. You can challenge the police officer's view of what happened, and even though you may think cops are looked at as the final letter of the law, it is possible to eradicate this belief in numerous ways.

You can challenge an officer's interpretation of the law. If the officer was in no position to view the crime effectively, if they had to drive around 50 miles per hour to reach the area of the infraction, you can argue that their conclusion could not be made clearly.

If they argued that you made an unsafe left turn, you might be able to get out of this charge by proving why your turn was indeed safe under the circumstances and in the situation that you were in.

In a variety of circumstances, you can find the reason why the cop's interpretation may be incorrect or why they were not positioned in a good spot to realize the full scope of the crime or of the infraction indicated. If this is the case, you will have a good chance of beating the ticket.

In many states, the speed limit is not established as an absolute restriction on how fast a person may or may not go, but simply as a presumption of the safe speed. If an officer pulls you over because you are going faster than the suggested limit, you may be able to prove that your speed was not unsafe or too fast.

2. **Challenge the officer's observations**

In addition to charging when the officer interpreted as happening, you can also challenge what the officer saw, or what they though they saw. In this case, the observations must be objective, and if it can be proven that the observations are not steeped in fact, are not objective or can be misinterpreted, you may be able to get out of your ticket for a variety of simple reasons.

The laws should not be made on judgment calls, like a play in basketball or baseball made by a referee, but should follow set guidelines and restrictions. If you do not feel that an officer as done this, you can do something about it by challenging the ticket.

If you can make a judge believe you instead of the officer in some situations, you can easily win your case.

If you were ticketed for failing to make a complete stop, the ticket can be fought if you can prove that the police officer's observation was incorrect. There are a number of things that you can do to provide information that you are right and the law officer is wrong in this particular case, or this particular offending situation.

These include:

-statements of witnesses
-pictures or diagrams
-models of the scene of the violation
-any other evidence that could cast doubt on the officer's observations

If there were witnesses, other passengers or other bystanders near the scene of the violation, you can use their word or their proof to prove that you made that complete stop or to prove that the turn you made was not illegal or not unsafe.

You could also use pictures and diagrams that show why you are not at fault, and that why the things that you did were not particularly illegal, unsafe, dangerous or against the law. You can also use these things to prove why you may not have been at fault in the situation in question.

Photographs or videos can also definitively prove that you did or did not do what you are charged with doing.

Likewise, you can use diagrams or real life demonstrations that show off obscure stop signs, hidden signals or low hanging branches that may have prevented you from fully knowing that what you were doing was illegal.

3. "Mistake of fact"

If you can prove that your violation was simply a mistake of fact – that is, if it was an honest or reasonable lapse in judgment or mistake in action – you may be able to have the ticket dismissed immediately.

Many judges will use leeway in these situations, and if you have a good record and a good personality, it will further help you to have these kinds of charges dismissed. There are a variety of circumstances that can prompt this response, and this will give you the freedom to enjoy a reprieve from the ticket.

These can come in a variety of situations. Some of these might include:

-Failing to stop before a crosswalk because the paint was washed away
-Failing to slow down because a sign was hidden after a storm
-Failing to slow for a sign because it was new

Also, almost any speeding tickets can be listed as a mistake of fact because the signs may not have been clearly marked and the sign may have been placed in an area to fool you by the sudden presence of a sign in a tricky location.

4. Legally justified conduct

If your conduct was legally justified, even if speeding illegally, you can get out of a ticket under the right circumstances. The circumstances might determine that your violation was not illegal, not dangerous, not unsafe or not against the spirit of the law.

This can happen for a variety of reasons, and you can get out of a variety of different speeding tickets for these reasons.

If you were driving too fast, it may have been to avoid an accident you saw coming. You may have sped up to more easily get through a yellow light, which may have been a much safer option than slamming your brakes and stopping abruptly.

You may have been driving too slow to make a lawful turn, or you may have increased your speed to get out of a car's blind spot. You may have sped up to clear the way for an emergency vehicle, or may have increased your speed slightly to allow for some other odd circumstance.

Other situations may have had you speeding because you felt a health condition coming on, and were trying to get to a nearby doctor's office, gas station or house.

You may have increased your speed for the justified reason that a hornet flew into your car, or because your wife is going into labor. You may have changed lanes too quickly because you felt it was the only safe way to avoid a traffic accident or situation.

These should raise facts and legal points in court, and should not be simply used to contradict an officer's legal points or their testimony. The facts should prove that what you did was not with malicious intent or that it was not on purpose.

5. Prove that you were avoiding harm or being safe

Even when you are doing something illegal, you may be doing it with the best intentions in mind or at heart. If this is the circumstance, you may be speeding to avoid an accident, avoiding harming another person or avoid a dangerous driving situation.

These emergencies are the most solid when the emergency is not of your own making, and you are simply reacting to a situation that can be dangerous or potentially harmful.

This is often a balance of risks, rewards and situations, and you must prove that you were violating the wording of the law to avoid a situation where another law is broken or another person is injured.

You might be speeding from the right lane if you are boxed into the lane and you are trying to get out of the way of a car merging onto the highway. You also might have to avoid being rear ended by a car that might not be paying attention. This can put you in a situation where you will have to speed up to avoid being hit – you will then be thus avoiding a dangerous situation where you might get hit or a more serious violation is committed by either you or the other driver.

You might find yourself speeding in a number of these situations, and all of the situations provide a legal reason to why you sped. And this legal reason might be the thing that prevents you from getting a ticket or a citation from a police officer.

Fighting the tickets in court

When you are in court trying to fight these tickets, you will have to have the right things with you to ensure that you are ready to beat the ticket and remove the citation from your record.

You will need a copy of your driving record and you will have to have your ticket and all other information given to you by the police officer at the scene of the incident.

There are a variety of options available to you that can allow you to get the judge to either eliminate the ticket or give you a lesser sentence, instead or your ticket or in addition to your ticket.

You can ask the judge to consider driving school or training instead of a ticket, and you can give yourself the opportunity to negotiate any other type of plea bargain.

These plea bargains can give you the opportunity to have one ticket dropped if you plead guilty to another ticket. If you plead to one ticket, perhaps a lesser ticket, the judge may accept because they will then not have to represent the case against your other ticket.

You might be able to simply give the judge a reason to excuse your ticket. You can prove your character or driving record, or treat the court cordially to give yourself a chance of not being hit with the highest level of the ticket.

Hiring an attorney is another option, but this may be an expensive option. If you can find an attorney with a low fee per job or per hour, you may be able to finish your case quickly, and reap some long-term savings.

While you may end up spending more than the price of the ticket, this can benefit you as you will not have to suffer increased auto insurance prices and you will not have to work with extra points on your license for years. These are all viable options to fighting that ticket that you have been dreading.

About Minute Help

Minute Help Press is building a library of books for people with only minutes to spare. Follow @minutehelp on Twitter to receive the latest information about free and paid publications from Minute Help Press, or visit minutehelpguides.com.